JUST KEEP
A BAG
PACKED

JUST KEEP A BAG PACKED

A Memoir

Edna Carr Green

authorHOUSE®

AuthorHouse™
1663 Liberty Drive
Bloomington, IN 47403
www.authorhouse.com
Phone: 1-800-839-8640

Published by AuthorHouse   01/21/2013

ISBN: 978-1-4817-8196-1 (sc)
ISBN: 978-1-4817-8197-8 (e)

Contents

I am dedicating this book to the two people who said they would buy it if I wrote it, Deb Krebsbach and Michael Bourdeaux with many thanks.

CHAPTER 1

1960

I THINK I have to make it clear here that the 1960's compared to today were rather like the Middle Ages. There were no mobile phones and most people though twice about using the phone because it was expensive. Telephone calls went through an operator who would frequently listen in. There was no way of communicating other than by phone or letter and most people wrote letters which could take some time to be delivered if it was Continent to Continent. There was no internet available to everyone. I have to say this because if I was reading my memoirs I would perhaps think why didn't they just sent an email or telephone. So please try to believe in a world where people were cut-off from each other to a much greater extent.

It all began when I got married; actually, it all began when I thought about getting married. I was never sure marriage was a good idea, and the more I thought about it the less I liked it, but it was 1960 and there was a lot of pressure. Living together was still living in sin and frowned on. God or fate or something read my mind and laughed. From the moment I tied the knot thunderbolts were thrown. I went into marriage thinking that if it didn't work out there was always divorce. But for the next thirty years there was always a crisis that moved that possibility to the back burner.

The Chinese curse 'May you live in interesting times' rumbled through my brain on a regular basis.

I was born and grew up in that usually derided and overlooked pocket of the British Isles known as Northumberland. I also grew up in the 1950s, when the whole of the UK was pretty drear, and the North the dreariest of all. Even potatoes were rationed—that's how bad it was. Consumers were trying to buy potatoes, not the latest fashion item or some new piece of software. It was not like Russia, but close.

So in 1956 I moved to London, shared a mews flat in Regent's Park, and really enjoyed my life there.

London was enormous fun and a million miles from the gloom of the North. However, towards the end of 1959, the company I worked for was taken over, the lease on the flat was up, and the girl I shared with was getting married, so it was time to go home, where my mother was always pleased to see me. A nice break for Christmas, then come back to London in the new year, look for a job and a flatmate, and start afresh.

While I was at home another escapee from the North, who had managed to escape farther than I had—to Singapore and Baghdad among other exotic places—came home.

We had known each other for ten years and had been part of the same group, although I was quite a bit younger.

There was really no talk of marriage, and I can't claim wild, impassioned love on either side, but we liked each other and had been friends for years. Neville needed a wife, and I was between jobs. Also, he agreed to my kind of wedding. In later years I constantly met men who admitted that after a three- or four-year posting overseas in some remote area of the world, they came home on long leave determined to find a wife. This accounts for some of the strange marriages we encountered, but most of them lasted a lifetime.

I knew that if I had to go through the whole white wedding business it would never happen. I had experienced my sister's wedding and wanted none of it. So we agreed to go on holiday to Spain and marry by special license; and that was really the start of it all.

Our parents, of course, did not believe we would really do it. The thought of anyone marrying abroad was beyond their comprehension. My sister had married in church, in white, with all the usual trimmings.

We drove off on a cold February morning in a 1960's Ford Consul convertible and the colour was 'sunburst yellow'. It rained all the way down the A1 from Newcastle to the first stop just north of London the first day, and it drizzled all the way across the Channel to France. We crossed the Pyrenees in blinding snow, a condition for which the Consul convertible was not suited, and we slithered very close to the edge of the road on many occasions. We also bickered all the way to Spain, our final destination.

In 1960 the roads in Europe were not crowded. We rarely saw a British number plate; in fact we rarely saw another car outside the cities.

We checked into the Hotel Inglaterra on the Paseo de Gracias in Barcelona and then went to the British Consul and asked him to perform a marriage ceremony. A voice from the back room said, 'And why do *you* want to get married?' It seemed like a rather rude question until the questioner appeared and turned out to be John, a friend of Neville's, recently posted to Barcelona.

It turned out that they did not dish out special licenses on demand no matter what Neville thought. We were going to have to spend three weeks in the Districts of Barcelona while notices were published. So we spent a few days in Barcelona while John showed us all the best restaurants. Then we decided, for economic reasons, to move out to the Costa Brava. Unfortunately, in those days the Costa Brava closed down between November and March. Even the post office boxes shut up shop, which proved to be something of a problem.

Eventually we found a small hotel run by a family who were bored and offered to open up for a couple of weeks. So we explored the area, practised our Spanish, learned all about tourist Spanish food, and killed time. We spent quite a bit of time searching for English Marmalade because breakfast was unendurable for Neville without Marmalade. Fortunately we found a version, of course the Spanish invented the original. During our whole three weeks we never saw another English person to speak to. Occasionally we saw a British number plate and occasionally parked next to one but, a smile from me produced the same result as that of an axe murderer, so we made no contact. This is not the only time I have had this reaction from Brits abroad.

After three weeks we returned from the coast and checked into the Hotel Inglaterra again. I made a quick visit to the hairdresser, then we took a taxi to the British Consul—not without difficulty, because the taxi driver first had to find out where it was. Eventually we were led up to the Consul's office where a pleasant if disapproving man greeted us. His first words after 'hello' were to the effect that he had paid for the flowers on his desk himself. Then he asked if his daughter could be present because she was off 'to do this sort of thing next week' in Mexico,

Edna Carr Green

and he wanted her to see it for herself. Ten minutes later it was all over, and as my husband has repeatedly pointed out over the years, I did not even take off my white leather coat. And so we went to lunch with John and one of the Consulate secretaries, which took around four hours.

CHAPTER 2

THE NEXT MORNING, fairly bright and early, we set off for the south of France. It was quite a long drive, but we got to Nice for a glamorous honeymoon. The sun shone, and we found a pleasant small hotel on the Promenade des Anglais and got set to enjoy our honeymoon. This was an age before credit cards, and all forms of credit were disparaged. Neville had sent a letter to his bank from the Costa Brava asking them to transfer funds so we could draw on them in France. We did not know that post office boxes were not opened on the Costa Brava between November and March, mail inside just stayed inside. The boxes were not sealed so Neville's letter to his bank just sat there with many other letters no doubt until Spring.

Apart from that, it was so far so good — too good — time for fate to wag a finger. We were woken very early the next morning by the hotel manager saying the police wanted us to contact them because my mother was ill.

When registering with an hotel, passports were checked, forms were filled and sent each night to the local policestation. There were few tourists in March 1960 so they knew who was staying where immediately. In a rather shattered state we went to to the police station, where they told me it was my *bonne mere*, or mother-in-law, who was ill. They allowed us to phone home where I discovered it was in fact my father who had suffered a severe heart attack and might or might not recover. So that was the end of the honeymoon. I still entertain the possibility that our telegram saying we were married caused his heart attack, but I really think not. He was never well and had suffered from a duodenal ulcer as long as I could remember. He was not accepted for the army because he was unfit and was drafted into the auxiliary fire service where he suffered a concussion or maybe worse; I was still a child at the time. I do know he spent several months in hospital and then went to live near Nottingham for a few years, paying us visits once in a while. So I think news of my marriage was not traumatic enough to bring on a heart attack.

We packed again and drove as far as Lyons, being waved down by countless gendarmes who had been told to look out for our car. A bright yellow Ford with English number plates in the south of France in March in 1960 was easy to spot.

We parked the car outside a large hotel and, feeling totally exhausted, went to sleep. When we came down in the morning the car had of course been broken into, easy with a convertible; and all my luggage—Neville's was in the boot—was gone. Fate was obviously interested in me. The thieves didn't steal the car or tackle the boot. I was left with nothing but the clothes I had worn the day before. My suitcase also contained all my jewellery, not that it was expensive but it had history and so I was not thinking straight and had never having been robbed before was not anticipating it. So with nothing but the clothes I has worn the day before, a visit to the local gendarmerie was necessary if I wanted to file a claim on my insurance.

I was taken into an office by a a very nice gendarme, and between his English, my French, and a good deal of sign language we managed to make a report. Absolutely necessary if I was to claim on insurance. Some of my clothes and stuff were found later on the central reservation of a nearby motorway I was told. I decided I did not want them back. After completing the necessary forms etc. Neville and I left for Montargis and hopefully from there a relatively easy drive to Calais and a ferry to cross the Channel. Unfortunately, while we were driving through the narrow streets of the town, first a grinding then a clanking sound emerged followed by a sudden stop and black smoke from the engine. Chaos ensued because no one could pass and we couldn't move. Eventually a breakdown truck appeared and towed us to a garage. They took a look and said some sort of plug had come loose on this brand new car, and all the oil had drained out. The engine had completely seized up. There would have to be a new engine, and it would take a while. So we tried to call the

Automobile Association (AA). But it was Saturday afternoon and it was 1960, so there was no reply.

So far the marriage was not going too well. Three days and three problems, a father very ill, most of my best clothes and jewellery stolen, and finally no transport.

We arranged to leave the car there and took a taxi to the local railway station so we could get a train to Paris. On arrival at the station I enquired about the briefcase containing all useful documents. A stricken look appeared on Neville's face, and he retraced is steps. Fortunately the briefcase was where he had left it. At least we still had our passports.

So we took a train to Paris, and had no problems with luggage because there wasn't much left. We had no other problems either, once the taxi driver had grabbed me as I got out of the car and pointed out that traffic ran from left to right in Paris rather than right to left as in the UK so the passing car missed me. I suppose he had had problems with tourists before.

Sunday morning we had a whole day to kill on less than 100 francs, which meant we consumed lots of sidewalk coffee. My French was schoolgirl and Neville's was worse. In those days the French attitude was—and I quote: 'If you don't speak French don't come to France'; and almost everything was closed on Sundays.

On Monday morning the banks opened, when Neville could make arrangements for funds. The AA was also in business. We had money, we could go home, and the AA promised to sort out the car. We took a train and ferry to Dover, and a train to London to buy a change of clothes and make more phone calls home. My father was improving, but slowly, so we took the next train home and got back to a house shrouded in gloom.

My mother was always very dramatic. She was upset but wearing her oldest clothes and playing tragedy to the hilt;was not helping and my sister, who had come home to be supportive, was at the end of her tether. It may sound hard to say this, but my mother left my father on various occasions and had affairs during the whole of their married life.

I've never seen the virtue of constantly telling everyone how worried you are. My mother was always telling me how worried she was about me. Whenever I wanted to do anything of which she disapproved she said it was 'too worrying'. So I try not to worry because worrying achieves nothing. I either try to fix something or move on.

I visited my father, who was in fact getting on pretty well. I sent my mother and my sister to the hairdressers and sorted out the house. I dragged them out to the cinema and shopping. My sister needed to go home to her own husband, and my father recovered enough after a couple of weeks to come home too. He was OK. He couldn't work anymore and had to lead a quiet life, so he was bored out of his mind. But he took long walks and read lots of books and survived another couple of years. In fact he lived long enough to see Jeremy born, which was nice; he had always wanted a son.

So the rest of Neville's leave was taken up ferrying my father to hospital and trying to put a brave face on things. My Dad was only fifty-six, but this was 1960, and there was not much that could be done for him.

Along came May, and the time had come to leave. The bank had decided that the fleshpots of the Far East were not for us. We said goodbye to both sets of parents and set off for Beirut. Neville would learn Arabic at The Middle East College for Arabic Studies or MECAS as it was known which was at that time operating in the village of Shemlan a village in the hills south of the city of Beirut.

CHAPTER 3

BEIRUT IS THE capital of Lebanon, a country which has had more than its share of troubles since 1975. After the end of World War I it was placed under the French Mandate, so when we arrived it was still a very French city. It was a major tourist and banking haven, especially for the Persian Gulf oil boom. It was a city where anything was possible, I discovered, and discretion was an important part of the package.

We boarded a BOAC Comet at Heathrow, which was then all corrugated buildings and fairly small and quiet. Bank officers at all levels flew first class in those days. Most lady passengers wore dresses, high heels, and often gloves. Men wore suits and ties, everyone was very polite, and jeans were never seen. We boarded and were served morning coffee followed by lunch, afternoon tea, and dinner. Of course we landed more than once, and it was a much longer flight than today. When we landed at Beirut it was quite a shock to my senses. It was hot, noisy, smelly, and confusing—in fact a very Middle Eastern city. Neville had described it as a very sophisticated city, and it was, but not in the way that I expected.

Young men employed by the Chartered Bank of India, Australia, and China—and they employed only young men—did tours of duty. Their first tour was four years, and during this time they were not allowed to marry. After four years they were given six months leave. The bank had been established in 1853, when everyone travelled by ship, and it took months to get to and from the UK. Even in the 1950s an officer could opt to go home by sea, and many people did. Six months in the UK with a wife and family, often having to rent a house, was not everyone's idea of heaven.

The bank did not want any shipboard romances, and when there was any sign of a young man getting too close to a girl, especially a local girl, he was immediately reminded of the terms of his contract and posted to the other side of the world. After the first tour, and providing he was over twenty-eight years old, if the officer wanted to marry, he was required to produce his fiancée so that senior management could look her over. If she was not regarded as suitable, he too was posted to the back of beyond, indicating that he should resign. If he did not take the hint, he could spend the next twenty-five years in pretty grim places.

Neville had done two tours and was in his early thirties when we married, and it seems I had passed muster, so we were set.

He had to do a takeover when we arrived in Beirut. This was bank practise and a security thing. This meant that we had to live in a hotel for four weeks until his predecessor went on leave. The hotel was just off Rue Hamra, and not far from the apartment we would occupy when Neville had fully taken over his job. According to recent news, Rue Hamra is now the centre of Hezbollah activities in Beirut, but it was quiet when we lived there. I often wonder who is living in the flat now, but they probably don't worry about the cockroaches as much as I did.

Neville left at 8:00 a.m. every morning and returned around 4:00 p.m. for lunch. He worked Middle East hours, the idea being that everyone took a nap in the afternoon so they could go out and party at night. Not the British way, but fine once you got used to it.

The cocks didn't seem to know that they were supposed to crow only at daybreak, and made music all night outside our window, or so it seemed. The ceiling of our bedroom was a playground for geckos—and I was told that their shit was poisonous if it came anywhere near your food or drink—and at our feet the large, overweight cockroaches scavenged rather loudly for whatever they could find, and of course cockroaches can live on anything. These were not the small, delicate cockroaches one might find in

England. I never saw one of these in the whole of my life until I came to Beirut; they were a couple of inches long and black and shiny and crunched when you stood on them.

The days were long because I knew no one and was reluctant to explore the narrow streets full of the kind of men I had seen only in Hollywood crime movies and black-clad women. I didn't dare go out in case I got lost and could not find my way back to the hotel; I still have no sense of direction, and I panic when I am lost. Beirut was a world of broken pavements and strange sounds and smells, and no one spoke English. I looked from the bedroom window at a confused arrangement of buildings, mostly half-finished in case their owners decided to put on another story; and there seemed no logic to any of it. If I ventured into those back streets I decided I would never be seen again and would be on my way to some foreign harem. All quite ridiculous but coming from England my mothers tales of the white slave trade termporarily overcame my rationality. That and too many bad movies, I'm afraid.

In reality, the Lebanese were always very kind and helpful; and they usually spoke bad French exactly like mine. When I went into a shop they would say '*Salaam Aleikum*' in Arabic, and then 'You are welcome', usually in English. Everybody seemed to be tri-lingual in Arabic, French, and English. They were charming, amusing, and always helpful, but I didn't know that when I arrived.

We finally moved into the top-floor flat that was to be our first home. It was a comfortable flat, light and airy, with marble floors and the minimum of furniture, but a bigger quota of cockroaches than the hotel. When the elevator reached our floor, an overhead light came on, and the floor became alive with a retreating army rushing for cover. But not nearly as fast as I ran for the front door of the flat, because I knew there were fewer cockroaches inside. I was terrified of all kinds of bugs and roaches. When I lived at home, we called my father if a beetle dared to make an appearance on the staircase. When I shared a flat with a girl in London, we discovered a mouse in the kitchen, and just shut the door for three days and hoped it would find better pickings somewhere else — and it did. Girls living in flats were not big on cooking even in the 1950s. Now it seemed I lived in a world of entomology, and once in bed would not move because I knew an army of bugs was waiting for me.

There was no air-conditioning, of course, and Beirut in the summer is very hot. Neville's working hours continued to be long, and so were the days. There were few European wives, and they were all busy with small children. Of course the elegant Lebanese ladies thought we were all unkempt and boring. But I needed company, and a dog seemed the safest option, so I said I needed a dog. In the end I became the owner of a dachshund puppy.

Nagi (meaning 'one who was saved' in Arabic) was a dog of great character, even if he was small, and a source of great amusement over the few years we had him. Nagi was always being saved because he was always in trouble. He found Beirut streets too hot for his feet and sat firmly on his bottom after putting one paw on the pavement if I wanted to take him for a walk. The only alternative was to carry him around in my shopping basket so he could just put his head out, and he found this much more acceptable. He also did not like being left alone when we went out at night; and he discovered how amusing it was to grab the end of the toilet roll in the guest bathroom and to run around and around the furniture until it ran out.

CHAPTER 4

BEIRUT WAS DIFFERENT. Lebanon is a Mediterranean country with blue skies and lots of outdoor living—different from the grey skies and chilly dampness that seemed to cover most of England during the 1950s. The fruit and flower markets showed an explosion of colour I had never seen before. The fruit sellers insisted that I taste fruit before buying it. The fruit was huge, and there was a vast choice. In England I was not even allowed to touch it. And I had never seen such an array of flowers. Not neat little bunches, but huge arrays bursting with bright colours. It wasn't paradise, but it was interesting, and the natives were friendly. Because of the climate everything started early, and then during the heat of the day everything died. Come dark the streets thronged and shops and restaurants stayed open till the small hours. In 1960 in London, shops closed at 5:00 p.m., and by six thirty Oxford Street was empty. Saturday everything closed at 1:00 p.m., and nothing opened on Sundays. The centre of London was a ghost town.

Apart from Europe, which was still war-torn in the late 1950s, I knew nothing of the world and assumed it was all like the UK. I could not have been more wrong.

We did buy a car, a broken-down, small, old Renault, which Neville promptly had resprayed sunburst yellow. We didn't use it much in Beirut, but once we moved to Shemlan we needed a car. The only way of getting around other than by private car was by Service Taxi. I don't remember any buses, although I'm sure there must have been some. The Service Taxis were large, old Mercedes which took five passengers and appeared to pick up and put them down anywhere. There must have been a set route, and one had to be patient because if the passenger in the middle of the back seat wanted to get out twenty yards from the place the last passenger exited, everyone had to shuffle around again.

Our stay in Beirut was to be short. Neville had been told that in September we were moving to Shemlan, a village in the nearby mountains, so he could study Arabic. Friends told him he should try to get a start on the language since it was very difficult, especially for someone who had no previous ability with languages. This meant that Neville finished work every Saturday afternoon at 4:00 p.m., and every Sunday morning he left after an early breakfast to drive up to Shemlan to start his studies with a private tutor. That was the theory. When I finally got to Shemlan I got the impression there had been a lot of background, namely chatting and drinking, but not much actual studying. So the four months I spent in Beirut were not the most enjoyable — largely my fault, I expect. I should have been much more adventurous.

I did, however, learn to cook in Beirut. I brought with me *Mrs. Beeton's Book of Cookery and Household Management*. It was a lifesaver even though I later discovered the author was a terrible cook who died before she had done much household managing. However, the book assumed the reader knew nothing about food and even included diagrams showing which part of the cow, sheep, and pig the various cuts of meat come from. But of course the ingredients found in grocery shops in the UK and the way meat was cut by butchers in Beirut were different. Alas, there was also no Bisto, which was the backbone of my gravy at that stage. I didn't know much about cooking rice, which was big in local dishes, my only experience being the rice pudding served up by my mother on a regular basis, which I hated as a child and still remember the struggle when I was being forced to try it. My grandmother insisted that no child could dislike rice pudding and tried various forms of disguise to convince me that I was just being difficult. Mrs Beeton was not good on rice, apart from rice pudding, which I can honestly say I have never cooked.

I learned to give dinner parties with three courses, and who must sit where, and which wines must be served when. These were not like the dinner parties I gave with the girl I shared a flat with in London, when the young men were so delighted to be invited to dinner that they would sit around our cramped table praising everything to the skies. Here it was all pretty formal, with the wives checking out the cooking and the table setting of the newly arrived bank wife.

Things improved when Jane Black, the wife of the branch manager, returned from America. I always found Americans more helpful than the English. She showed me around a bit, and I discovered how pleasant the Lebanese were. The fruit and flower markets were fantastic, and I found a maid who cooked and cleaned much more efficiently—and quickly—than I ever could, even when the temperature was not over a hundred degrees. We started to make friends and went out to some of the great restaurants that were plentiful and cheap. Lebanese wine cost 2/6d (about 12 pence) a bottle, and champagne was 5/—(25 pence).

CHAPTER 5

Eventually, in September, we moved up to Shemlan and into a small flat high on the hills behind Beirut overlooking the airport but close to the school. When we moved in, the days were still warm, and we sat on the balcony and enjoyed the views, watching the planes landing at the airport below after flying in over the sea. Neville's fellow students were mostly around our age if they were from oil companies or banks, and there were a few academics, but the largest contingent by far was from the Foreign Office, including students. These were young men away from home for the first time who were always hungry and usually arrived for a visit around lunchtime. By then I had learned to cook. There were of course some very smart young people on the course. David Gladstone, a descendant of a British Prime Minister, regularly drove down to Beirut. William Lancaster, the son of a famous cartoonist who drove all the way from the UK in a hearse. There were some rather wild and wonderful couples who worked for oil companies, such as Trudi and Louis Wesseling. And of course George Blake, the spy who, it later turned out, had spent most of his time down in Beirut with Philby and friends.

The students studied in small groups of three, but other than that they divided themselves naturally into the young and wealthy, who rushed down to Beirut wearing dinner jackets every weekend for 'debauchery', which usually meant eating, drinking and gambling; and the young marrieds, who had to make do with drunken dinner parties. The rest just spent the weekends trying to catch up on their homework.

MECAS ran courses for the wives, telling us things about local hygiene, and to be sure all fruit and vegetables were soaked in Daz washing machine powder, as it had been discovered this killed everything. We were told some of the fertilizers used in the growing of these were suspect. Lettuce was not recommended, as it was mostly water anyway. Of course it was also important to rinse everything off after buying it, and everything had to be well cooked.

They also ran a wives course to teach us colloquial Arabic two afternoons a week. We were not taught to read written Arabic or how to write it. We started off with greetings, whereupon I discovered that Arabic greetings are very special. To every opening 'hello'—not that they ever say that—there is a special response. I think I counted ten different greetings with their responses and wondered how long it took before they got to conversation. It does, of course, mean that conversations are rarely rushed. Everyone has time to reflect on the meeting, and by the time the greetings are finished, has weighed up the situation. We also learned the words we might need to instruct servants and buy food. All this did come in very useful later on in Abu Dhabi and in Tripoli, Libya.

Then came winter, and the old saying about skiing in the mountains in the morning and sunbathing on the beach in the afternoon became at least partially true. We had lots of snow and lots of frost, even though we were not at skiing height. The flat was freezing, and the only form of heating the flat was a *mazout* stove in the living room which burned paper bags filled with some kind of treated wood shavings. This also heated the water, eventually. Nagi hated the cold and spent most of his time curled up on my lap sharing my quilt. He also had a bad habit of jumping out of the car window as we approached home long before the car stopped. Cars were not air-conditioned in those days, so it was a feat to remember to close the car windows when we were getting close to home, and it was a miracle that he did not break a leg or get run over by another car.

I drove up and down to Beirut to do my shopping on Rue Hamra because there was a supermarket there and a nice coffee shop. There were lots of clothes, much too expensive for our budget, but lovely to window-shop. Shemlan boasted a tiny grocery, and that was the only shop. I think the village existed totally on income from the MECAS school.

So we started learning Arabic—Neville the whole business of classical language and the written script, and I joined the rest of the wives learning the colloquial stuff, suitable for conversation and marketing. We had Christmas in Shemlan since we could not afford to go away as some of the students did, and cut our Christmas tree from the many growing wild on the hillside. It was quite biblical in the small church where we attended midnight Mass, freezing cold with totally clear skies filled with stars.

CHAPTER 6

——

THEN CAME THE spring, when I should have been feeling lively, but instead I began feeling sick and listless. Having been told by my doctor in the UK that I would probably find it difficult to become pregnant, I discovered it was not difficult at all, even with precautions.

Neville found it so difficult to believe, he sent me back to the doctor twice. We had never discussed having a family, and now it was too late. I had never given it any thought, and I doubt if Neville had; and neither of us was too sure about it, except it added another complication to our lives.

Neville's salary barely covered our living expenses once we had paid for the rental of the flat. This was not unusual with overseas banks at that time.

It was fifteen miles down a twisty mountain road to Beirut where the hospital was, and Neville was no keener to drive it with a wife in labour than I was to have him drive me. Apart from the fact that it was a narrow, twisty road with a steep drop on one side and a rock wall on the other, Lebanese drivers always felt the safest place to be was in the middle of the road straddling both lanes. And they were right, but it did mean that everyone played 'chicken', which was bad enough in daylight, but suicide in the dark. There were always a lot of accidents.

I had always managed to avoid all information on the business of having babies. Doing so was easy in the 1950s. At school I regularly fainted in biology classes and decided that the subject was not for me.

Going home to mummy solved our financial problems, because living as a student in school was cheap, and Neville felt he would be able to study better without baby complications. But there was the problem of Nagi, too, of course. If Neville lived in school, what would happen to my best companion Nagi? Fortunately, friends with a Labrador loved Nagi and offered to look after him while I was away.

So I flew home in April, but just before I flew we had a visiting general manager, Louis Goldsmith, telling us about our next posting: Abu Dhabi.

I said that I was about to leave for the UK to have the baby, and he voiced his disapproval. I also suggested it might be better if I let Neville get settled in Abu Dhabi, which was not in Wales, as everyone suggested, but in some foreign place that I — and the rest of the world at that stage — had never heard of. It also appeared that there was no accommodation for us in Abu Dhabi. There were no hotels, there were only about four expatriates living there, it is hard to understand today but short of erecting a tent on the sand we would not have had a roof over our head. But this did not deter the general manager. He thought I was being difficult. He insisted that the bank would not pay my airfare from Beirut to Abu Dhabi unless I flew with my husband. He had of course never been to Abu Dhabi, the only person who had been there was my husband and he had visited from Sharjah, the next State. Mr Goldsmith could not imagine a place where there were no hotels or at least guest houses. Simply refused to believe there were no roads or medical services. He found it incomprehensible like most people that a place like Abu Dhabi could exist. We would, of course, have to pay my fare to and from the UK, and any other expenses involving the baby, because 'the bank employs the husbands, not the wives'. This was the constant cry of management at that time. He pointed out that his wife had always had her children in local hospitals, usually Indian with British doctors, and had no problems.

He missed the point. Everywhere he had worked there had been hospitals and some sort of infrastructure. Everyone who visited Abu Dhabi in the early years admitted they had never lived anywhere quite like it. The Political Agency had a radio, and that was the only means of communication with the outside world.

There were no roads, no telephones, no newspapers, no doctors, no fresh food except fish, and getting that was becoming difficult because the fishermen had discovered they could make more money working for the oil companies.

Abu Dhabi was just a narrow stretch of sand with no real reason for its existence, until they discovered oil.

CHAPTER 7

At the end of April I went home not at all sure that I would return. I flew Air Liban, the cheapest flight we could find, which had the kindest cabin crew I have ever encountered. My mother met me at the airport and we took the train to Northumberland. And so I settled in, looking very large and feeling like a pregnant elephant, to wait out the six weeks before the baby was due.

The George Blake spy scandal certainly enlivened the first few days. It was difficult to believe. Blake, a regular member of our social circle, did not seem like a super-spy, rather closer to the perfect English gentleman in tweeds. Just a couple of weeks earlier, Blake had arrived rather late at a goodbye party given for me by Bob Davies and his wife Pamela, and now I began to wonder what had kept him.

He had a very sweet wife and two or three children. It was impossible to believe he was a master spy. Although rapidly convicted and sent to prison for forty-two years, he did not serve his sentence. In 1966 he scaled the outer wall of Wormwood Scrubs jail by using a homemade rope ladder, strengthened by ten pairs of size thirteen knitting needles. He may not have been British, but he chose a very British form of escape. A pink chrysanthemum left outside was apparently regarded as a clue as to who had helped George to escape — the Russians. It was rather more like a British comedy farce than the spy novels written about James Bond. It is hard to imagine all those all those knitting needles in Wormwood Scrubs. Of course, it had always been hinted that MECAS was a spy school, but this seemed to add weight to the rumour.

All this was a far cry from Monkseaton where I was staying with my mother. High tides and strong winds were the only excitement on this bleak Northumbrian coast.

But I still had a few weeks to kill, so I rented a little car and drove around the countryside and tried to be patient, not something that ever came easily. My father was better, but not allowed to work, so he spent his time taking walks and reading books and being bored, too.

Antenatal care was non-existent — no one suggested what I should or should not eat no warmings about alcohol, or that it was a good idea to take a walk rather than drive and keep my weight down. Fortunately I did not put on too much weight, but that was purely by chance. I visited the hospital every two weeks for them to have a look at the baby. Near the due date they kept saying to come back in a week if nothing happened. Nothing did happen, so when the baby was well overdue, they decided labour should be induced. I could not have been more pleased. If I had felt like an elephant before, by now I felt like a pregnant elephant. Even after my labour was induced, Jeremy was reluctant to be born, and I had begun to think I might be pregnant forever.

I lay there pretending to the best of my ability that nothing was happening, and finally Jeremy put in an appearance. He was eight and a half pounds of terror as far as I was concerned, because I knew nothing about babies, and he did look very small and vulnerable.

I was lucky; he was perfect, but he still cried a lot. I spent a week in a maternity home recovering and then faced looking after the baby myself. It was just as well my mother knew a bit about babies, and my sister had already presented her with three grandchildren, so she was good every time I panicked.

I could not fly for another six weeks while Jeremy had his fortnightly check-ups to see that he was progressing properly.

He was a very healthy baby, which was just as well, since I was about to take him to a place where there were no medical facilities at all.

After the six weeks were up I drove down to London with my mother; Jeremy was in a carrycot in the back. We had no seat belts then. I checked into a hotel at Heathrow and the next day boarded a plane for Beirut by the skin of my teeth. They had to put the stairs back and grab the carrycot. My hand luggage of baby equipment for the flight weighed twenty-two pounds. It was a long flight to Beirut in those days, and I needed every bit of it.

At the end of July the MECAS year ended. School was out, so Neville had booked us into a hotel in Beirut where we stayed for two days before catching a BOAC flight to Bahrain. I was going to have to stay in Bahrain for a short time until Neville found accommodation and a building in which to open a branch of the bank, as Sheikh Shakhbut bin Sultan Al Nahyan had demanded. Easier said than done.

CHAPTER 8

WE ARRIVED AT Bahrain airport at noon on 1 August 1961. The date was burned in my brain because it was 120 degrees in the shade according to the thermometer hanging on a bit of wood in the immigration shack. We had Nagi in a dog box and Jeremy in a carrycot. Looking around at the surrounding concrete I remembered the old saying about frying eggs on pavements. I swear it would have been possible had there been a pavement. The immigration area was simply a galvanised roof to keep off the sun. The line was not long because Bahrain was not a popular destination then, but in the short time we stood there the fly netting of the carrycot was black with flies.

Peter Rawlings, another junior bank officer, met us and took us to our flat, a large empty apartment above the bank. Then John and Bebe Lawrence gave us lunch and tried to be kind.

They had a flat next to ours, but much larger and well equipped, with views over the Indian Ocean. They lived a pretty civilised life with good servants, and most things were available in Bahrain at that time. There was a pretty large expatriate population since Bahrain was a base for both British and American forces. There was also Awali, a completely self-contained town for Americans who worked in the oil industry, with its own cinema and other amenities. Rumour had it that the Americans never actually went into Bahrain. When they arrived they took a company bus to the Awali compound and stayed there until they took a company bus to the airport to go on leave. They maintained there was nothing in Bahrain that was of any interest to them, and they had a point, but it was still rather sad. But there were enough expatriates living in Bahrain to make it worthwhile for the shops to stock anything that they might want or need, including everything I needed for the baby, such as milk, Milton baby products, and baby food. Dorabjee, the local grocery store, had it all. There were, of course, British doctors and nurses and hospitals, and a very good medical service. In fact it was a pretty easy place to live.

But our flat had been abandoned as a place for bank staff to live, so it contained only things that no one else wanted. A baby Belling cooker and a tiny fridge had been hurriedly installed in the kitchen along with an assortment of plates and cups and a kettle. The flat had two huge, dark bedrooms, a living room with two sofas and a standard lamp, and a dining room with a table and eight chairs. There were four rooms bisected by corridors wider than a cricket pitch, and all rooms were very dark, with thick walls and small windows, because the building had been built before air conditioning became normal. In fact, the air conditioning was very good—the same kind as used in freezer equipment, I was told. It had wide verandas running around the outside, which was bliss for Nagi, because he could run around and bark at the passers-by below until it got too hot for him.

So after a couple of days Neville left, and I had to work out how to shop for food and other items without taking Jeremy, since I had no pram, and anyway the flat was up a long flight of stairs. The things that mothers carry their babies in now had not been invented, and we had no servants. I could not leave him alone, and it was too hot and too difficult to carry him while I shopped. In the end Bebe came to my assistance and looked after Jeremy whilst I made lightning visits to the grocers.

At night Jeremy, Nagi, and I huddled in the large bedroom with the door locked in case some dastardly Arab tried to come in and slit our throats. All those old movies were still playing in my head.

Neville came back from time to time on weekends, and on one weekend we decided to have Jeremy christened. Canon Alun Morris, a Welshman, was the Vicar in charge of St. Christopher's Church, and we had a nice service which Neville almost missed because he always has to fit in just one more thing.

This time it was picking up a suit to wear at the christening.

The Lawrences hosted a large and very wet lunch in their flat after the ceremony. Somehow parties in Europe are never the same as those in the wilder places of the world.

For several weeks Neville commuted between Dubai, where he was trying to set up some sort of infrastructure, and Abu Dhabi, where he was trying to find a building for the bank and possibly somewhere to live. Eventually he was able to lease a building in the souk that the British Bank of the Middle East had vacated to move into a purpose-built accommodation. Unfortunately there were no empty houses; most of the local population lived in *barustis*, which were houses woven from palm fronds, cool and shady and requiring very little maintenance. Eventually, however, a friend from MECAS, Oliver Miles, Acting Political Agent, offered us a room in his flat above the office.

CHAPTER 9

So JOHN AND Bebe Lawrence drove me to the airport with Jeremy in his carrycot and Nagi in his basket. By now I had abandoned all vanity and wore a cotton dress and rubber flip-flops with my hair in a rubber band. Bebe pointed out that it was quite a change from my arrival in a linen suit, high heels, and a French pleat. Reality had changed my views. So we were loaded onto a Gulf Air Dove, a tiny plane that held about ten passengers. Once Jeremy's cot was wedged against the pilot's door there was no way he could leave us. Nagi was in the back of the plane with the tethered goat. The goat and Nagi were not sympathetic to each other and neither were keen on flying so it was rather noisy.

There were also a couple of Bedouin with hawks on their wrists. When the plane took, off so did the hawks, and this happened again when we landed at Doha. There was not a lot of traffic in the Gulf in

1961 — not enough to fill the tiny planes more than twice a week, in fact, so the airline was not too fussy about how it filled its seats.

We finally arrived in Abu Dhabi. The back door opened, and there stood Neville with his Land Rover at the bottom of the steps. There was no passport control and no airport of any kind, just another Land Rover and a windsock blowing in the wind.

I don't know what I expected. By now I just wanted to be settled *some*where — but it did look a bit like *no*where.

Abu Dhabi had survived on fishing and pearling to some extent. In 1958 the first oil was found, which totally changed the state of Abu Dhabi; but not much had changed yet when I arrived.

So now we were in Abu Dhabi with a Land Rover parked by the stairs from the plane. In September 1961 it was still very hot but in a way quite beautiful. Pure white sand stretched as far as the eye could see with no distractions apart from the odd palm tree and bit of scrub. The view was bounded far away across the flat white plain by shimmering turquoise sea. On the horizon was the ruler's palace, all very Lawrence of Arabia. There were no customs or passport controls because there was no airport. Just a windsock in the middle of endless sand.

Norman Turnbull ran the local branch of International Aeradio Limited which communicated with pilots wanting to land on the hardened sand strip known as Abu Dhabi airport by taking the battery out of his Land Rover and connecting it to some sort of ground-to-air system. The landing routine—I discovered later—usually consisted of a laconic: 'Everything all right up there?' 'Well everything seems to be OK down here, so you had better land then.' This is what I remember; these are memoirs after all, not sworn statements.

Once the pilot had landed, he climbed out and distributed little bags of mail—business letters, personal letters, the odd week-old newspaper, and on some days—heaven—a book or a magazine. There was no post office in Abu Dhabi either. As the months passed and the number of inhabitants increased, there would always be a little group of people sitting on folding chairs by the windsock, waiting for the mail. The arrival of mail was the highlight of the week, after all, so it deserved a proper reception from the whole community—there wasn't a lot to do in Abu Dhabi. Mail went out the same way. It was all a bit unreal. There was a rumour that a post office would open, and about a year later it did.

But this was all in the future. When I arrived, as far as I could see there was no one in sight except a few people unloading cargo and Neville with his Land Rover backed up to the door of the plane. Nor were there any roads, so Neville jammed his foot down firmly on the accelerator, something he still does, assuring me this was necessary, and we literally launched as fast as possible across very soft sand. I was later told Abu Dhabi has a special sort of sand, each grain perfectly spherical ground up shell, giving no purchase to tires. Jeremy in his carrycot was bounced right out of it by the corrugations in the sand, and Nagi was not impressed.

I soon learned that no one went out in a Land Rover without a shovel and a supply of old sacks in the back. We were constantly getting stuck in the sand, and digging out was a question of inserting sacks under the wheels. After that it was a question of one person driving and everyone else pushing. I pushed quite a few Land Rovers in my time, and even now when I see a vehicle stuck on TV, I am apt to give them advice loudly as to how to get out.

There was no available housing. At that stage Jean and Alan Horan, the oil company's representative, lived in what looked like a mansion; Jennifer and Alex Gillibrand, who ran the local branch of British Bank of the Middle East, had a perfectly good breeze block bungalow; the engineer who was building the new water filtration plant had a concrete hovel with an air conditioner; and the Political Agency had a flat above the office with two bedrooms and a living room. It was built to catch every breeze from the sea, and that helped.

We were lucky to be offered one of the bedrooms by Oliver Miles. So there we were: Neville, Jeremy, Nagi, and me, plus a million geckos, mice, and roaches—although I admit not as many roaches as Beirut, and they were smaller. Water was the greatest problem; it came from a local well and was less than pure and a bit salty. The Political Agency had arranged that four old kerosene cans were filled with water from a nearby well and had them strapped to a donkey. This was delivered every day and only once a day. If it ran out it was just bad luck. With a small baby this produced a few problems — especially with my lack of knowledge about babies.

There were, of course, no doctors, telephones, or roads — although soon a fleet of pickup trucks started bringing in subqa. This was a special sort of sand found in an area outside town and when treated could be laid to make a firm surface for cars and planes landing. They were building the first 'road', which ran from the old jetty past our house and the place that Grey McKenzie was building, past the British Bank of the Middle East house and a training school run for the oil company, then known as simply ADMA which was currently drilling on Das Island. It ended at the ADMA General Manager's house.

There were no childcare facilities; I'm not even sure the term had been invented in 1961. I had brought some tinned baby food from Bahrain, and for medical care I had to rely on the American baby guru Dr Spock and his book. In fact, the book often made things worse; it brought up problems I hadn't even thought of. Ignorance was undoubtedly bliss, but his advice always ended 'If you are worried, just consult your doctor or paediatrician', but the nearest doctor was a whole day's drive away in Dubai, and that was on a good day. It was, however, a lifeline in many ways, and it was a very well used copy that I finally abandoned.

We were there because oil money was beginning to flow into Abu Dhabi, and in the beginning it was packed into suitcases and flown from Bahrain and handed over to the ruler. He deposited with the British Bank of the Middle East, but when he decided to visit the bank one day and inspect his cash, they did a bad job of explaining that banks don't work that way, so the ruler asked for another bank, and since he had met Neville when he worked in Sharjah, the Ruler wanted him. In time, of course, the amount of money pouring into Abu Dhabi made it impossible for it to be loaded into suitcases, but by then the British Government had found all kinds of advisors for the Ruler who explained the banking system to him, and he no longer felt the need to see the actual notes.

After several weeks of living in the Agency flat and causing chaos all around, Oliver said we could move into the newly constructed prefabricated house that had been erected for an increase in staff. I believe not everyone was in agreement with him but it was certainly easier than coping in one room with nowhere to put the baby. The downside was that we had to accommodate and feed every passing visitor to the Agency as well as the Directors of some Companies who might want to bank with the Eastern Bank.

It was impossible to get servants because no one wanted to come to Abu Dhabi. So I had to do all the cooking and shopping in the souk. The worst part was learning to make bread, which definitely has a mind of its own. Neville thought he was doing me a favour when he bought a large sack of flour, which sat in a storeroom in tropical conditions. It became riddled with weevils, which was another bug I had never seen before. But I assumed all flour came with weevils and duly sieved them out before I made the bread. The first cook we managed to get looked at the flour and then, and threw it out with a look of disgust.

CHAPTER 10

THERE WERE MANY visitors to Abu Dhabi even in 1961, all wanting to put a spoon in the honeypot of money that came from the oil on which Abu Dhabi sat. They could be a blessing and a blast of fresh air or a curse because they wanted five star services. Some would arrive and on entering the house through the kitchen—the only possible way in because of the deep sand surrounding the house—would assume I was the cook. These tended to be 'important' Chairmen of Companies who had probably never been in a kitchen and certainly not one like mine. Their manners rapidly improved when they realised I was their only source of food and drink during their stay in Abu Dhabi. Especially drink. After a day of driving from Dubai where things moved fairly smoothly suddenly they were in non-airconditioned Land Rovers which got stuck constantly and though they did not have to get out and push they had to sit their in their suits dripping while other people did.

They spent time sitting in very hot Majlis and trying to do business. everyone needed a drink.

Dubai was the preferred place to work in the Persian Gulf; most people would rather have been there, especially domestic servants. That was the nearest source of civilisation, and regular visits were a necessity. But the road — in fact there was no road — just a sand track which was hard to follow. The Political Agency had to be advised before you left Abu Dhabi so that they could inform their opposite number in Dubai that you were en route. If you didn't turn up within a reasonable amount of time, the Trucial Oman Scouts were despatched. These were local men trained by British Officers. It was a bit like a British version of the French Foreign Legion but they were there to keep the peace not fight a war. There was no road to Dubai, just a track that the wind often covered with sand. People still got lost and died in the very hot conditions. And of course there was the *Muktah*, a boggy stretch of land run by the police to check on people coming and going. There was a short concrete causeway, but at high tide it was impossible to pass.

There was at least one occasion when I was grateful for the Trucial Oman Scouts, when someone tampered with our vehicle in Dubai and replaced the fuses with faulty ones. We had driven to Dubai with Jeremy to get the Land Rover serviced and do some much needed shopping. The vehicle just stopped halfway home in the middle of nowhere, and there was no way to contact anyone. We just had to wait for a passing vehicle. Fortunately, the passing vehicle belonged to the TOS, and like the US Cavalry, they rode to the rescue and fixed the vehicle.

We had to bring most of our supplies from Dubai, including—and especially—our supply of liquor. All Christians had a liquor license, but of course no liquor was available in Abu Dhabi. However, as the population grew, more and more people drove to Dubai, and because their vehicles were so heavy with crates of liquor, getting stuck in the sand became more frequent. One extra problem was that everyone would just settle down and lighten the load by drinking the beer until someone turned up to help them.

Dubai even then thought of itself as much more sophisticated than Abu Dhabi, and it was. It had an infrastructure with roads, telephones, fresh water, a creek to make it look picturesque, and shops selling fresh and tinned food. It had a large expatriate population because it had been a port for years and traded with the subcontinent of India and Iran. So it was cosmopolitan, with a Ruler who was determined to make his state wealthy and independent. In the 1960s Dubai was part of the Trucial States, which were presided over by the British, but Sheikh Rashid knew that his State was small, and then there was no sign of oil, so he had to make his money anyway he could. Even he could not have envisaged the Dubai that his sons have created today.

CHAPTER 11

EVENTUALLY WE HAD our very own prefabricated house with three small bedrooms, a living-dining room, two bathrooms, and a kitchen, which had a kerosene fridge and freezer. The freezer was like those old ice cream freezers: square, with thick walls and a handle on the top. It took up half the small kitchen. It was all constructed under the supervision of a huge Yorkshireman called Dennis Fulbrook, who lived in a caravan and spoke virtually no Arabic. He demonstrated his requirements to his Arabic-speaking labourers when there was a comprehension problem by grabbing them, shouting loudly and making violent gestures. If a panel was being installed upside down, the labourer was upended, and no further words were required. This might not go down well today, but then the workers just thought he was mad but funny and collapsed with laughter.

It was a very small house. The furniture was stuff I bought in Bahrain, had loaded on to the deck of a dhow, and shipped to Abu Dhabi. Unfortunately, the seas had been rough, with consequent damage, so when it arrived it was all in pieces, and a rather incompetent local carpenter had the job of sticking it all together. But at least we could sit down in a place we could call our own.

Our house was near the souk and surrounded by *barustis*, the homes of local families, and we overlooked the old jetty where the fishermen and all boats pulled up. It was right in the centre of town, but it was not noisy because then there were few vehicles, and apart from the odd donkey and the howls of the pye-dogs when there was a full moon, the only sound was that of the sea.

Later on we had a chain link fence, required by law to mark our boundaries, but in the beginning we were the latest attraction, especially with a blond baby. When I was not cooking in our tiny kitchen, with its kerosene fridge, freezer, and bottled gas cooker that left barely room for me, I was washing nappies in the bath to save water.

Occasionally I could actually settle down blissfully to read. At this point I would hear giggling, and looking up I would see half a dozen black-clad ladies peering in through their masks at my strange world of carpeted floor, bookcases, lamps, padded chairs, and tables. The house was just two meters away from the local families living in *barustis*, so we were certainly interesting to them. The other problem with prefabricated houses was that they came with wall unit air conditioners that were extremely noisy; they were efficient but it was like living in a submarine with windows.

We also had Nagi the dog, of course, who, despite all the stories about Arabs hating dogs, became quite popular with the locals. I think they liked his spirit. All the other dogs around were wild mixed breed salukis, at least twice his height, with legs long enough to cope with the deep sand, but Nagi was never deterred. Although we tried to keep him in our compound, it was quite impossible. As soon as the door was open, off he would go, chasing the females, with his little legs getting stuck in the sand, until some local would rescue him and appear on my doorstep curled up with laughter telling me of his exploits. Nagi was quite fearless, but unfortunately the increase in traffic meant his days were numbered.

The only wildlife I ever saw on land in Abu Dhabi were flies. No snakes, and no scorpions—those were saved for Libya. In the sea there were porpoises, one of which came right up to the edge of the beach. We followed it for some time before it got bored and took off into the deeper water. There are sharks also—but never at the same time as the porpoises, I was assured. I once saw something in the market which the locals called a *dugong*, which was about the same size as a porpoise, maybe seven feet long, and had a pointed snout.

We had a generator to make our own electricity to
run the window air-conditioning units and lights.
We discovered one night when the generator failed
that it also ran the lights of all the *barustis* around
us. I cooked on bottled gas, and kerosene ran the
fridge and freezer. I was also reliably informed that
prefabricated houses took less than three minutes to
burn to the ground, hardly consoling to someone with
a tiny baby and a house with no fire doors.

Because there were so few foreigners in Abu Dhabi
in 1961, whenever there was an Id (Moslem holiday),
I was welcomed by Sheikh Shakhbut into his majlis
when my husband paid his calls. It was a small, bare
room, oblong, with a couple of sofas opposite the
entrance and chairs lining both sides. If you were
lucky, you were beckoned to sit beside the Sheikh,
a charming man. You also got first go at the coffee
because a man with a coffee pot offered you a cup
with a tiny amount in the bottom. You had to drink
three cups, and then if you were wise or knew enough,
you waggled your cup and he moved on to someone
else with the same cups. He did give the cups a quick
swill out between customers but that was mostly to
get rid of the grains which were on the bottom. Arabic
coffee is very strong with a taste of cardamom, and
very sweet.

On reflection, we must have been of interest to the
whole village. There wasn't much to talk about. Abu
Dhabi was pretty isolated, and since I never heard a
radio in the early days, the problems of the rest of the
world got to us several days late.

Entertainment was non-existent. Eventually there was an occasional film, compliments of ADMA, the oil company, shown on the white painted side of their office. We plonked our chairs on the sand and watched a film projected onto the wall, drinking out of the flasks we had taken with us. All the locals, including the Ruler's daughter, if she had managed to avoid her police guard, sat on the sand in front of us, and by and large watched in amazement. These were the days long before the tentacles of television and the wonders of the Internet had reached the Gulf.

CHAPTER 12

I<small>T WAS CERTAINLY</small> a question of making one's own entertainment. Meanwhile, more people were arriving to live every day, and quite a few were families. As there were a couple of Scots, we pounded away at highland dances organised by Alistair Macaskill on his concrete patio or on his barge, where between dances you could watch the sea snakes ooze around it. The sound of loud highland music echoing over the desert didn't seem to bother the locals; of course some could say that Scottish music and Arabic music have a lot in common.

The population was rapidly expanding, so there were lots of 'parties', but that still left lots of lonely hours during the day. Neville left around 8:00 a.m., before it got too hot, and returned at 1:00 p.m. He went back around 4:00 p.m. and returned perhaps at 7:00 p.m., in time for a drink before dinner. Between 1:00 p.m.

and 4:00 p.m. everyone slept because it was too hot to move.

We took over someone's Indian ayah for a few months in late 1961 Her employer in Dubai said he couldn't stand her anymore, but I was desperate. At least it solved the babysitting problem. As far as I remember, Jeremy was the only expatriate baby in the town, so if we were invited to a party, he had to come in his carrycot and hopefully would sleep through. We still had not found anyone to cook or clean. Just before Christmas in 1961, Neville went off to Dubai to do some shopping and took Christine, the ayah, to give her a break, leaving me in the house alone. It was just for the weekend, and I didn't want to take the trip with Jeremy, who was still less than six months old. There was a knock on the back door in the afternoon of the day they left, and a man stood there with a telegram in his hand. This was quite impossible, because there was no telegram delivery service in Abu Dhabi, but there he stood with it in his hand, so I took it. It informed me that my father had died the day before, and I have to admit I never felt more alone. There I stood—in the middle of nowhere, with only my small baby for company and no possibility of contacting my mother or anyone else.

Eventually Christine went a little mad, as everyone did in the desert after a bit. She started tying cloves of garlic around Jeremy's neck because she said he was too beautiful and she must keep the evil spirits away.

There was also the occasion when the ever-boisterous Jeremy learned the joys of jumping on a bed. I was in the next room when there were screams and howls. Jeremy had slipped and cut his brow open. It was not Christine's fault; Jeremy was always getting into scrapes and has the scars to prove it. But she just collapsed into a howling heap, and Jeremy's cries could have brought down the rather insubstantial roof. There was blood everywhere, and it was hard to see what the real damage was. Neville turned white and rushed out of the room. There was no help for it other than the first aid box, so I closed the wound with tightly pulled Elastoplasts and held it there until the blood congealed. Later I asked another wife who had been a nurse what I should have done. I wanted to be prepared for the next drama. I told Christine perhaps it was time for her to look for another job, and she stalked out of the house. We looked everywhere for her and advised the police, since it was easy to die in the desert. After a week she reappeared all smiles, saying she had caught a lift to Dubai, and now she had another job.

The first Christmas arrived, and everyone tried to be festive. Bill Edge was the commandant of police. Rumour had it he rode around Abu Dhabi at night on his camel, a very imposing figure since he was a large man with a large baton so there was very little crime. Anyway, he brought his wife Ruby and his son out. Mike Daly brought his wife and children, and we invited one or two bachelors who were now beginning to be posted in by the oil companies. I gathered as many people as I could into our tiny pre-fabricated house, along with the food we had managed to get from Mr Bhojraj the man who ran the local shop, and a few things we got from Bahrain and Dubai. Mostly delicacies like cocktail sausages, cheese, nuts, anything to be found in a tin but nobody was fussy and no one was going to complain.

As the population grew, so did the number of 'parties', because that was almost the only form of entertainment. There was the occasional film, compliments of ADMA, the local oil company. This was shown on the whitewashed side of their office. We brought our chairs and plonked them on the sand and drank from our flasks while the locals, including the Ruler's daughter, if she had managed to avoid her police guard, sat in the sand in front of us and watched in amazement. The films were in English, of course, but that didn't seem to bother them. It was their first glimpse of the outside world.

It was very difficult to get books, which had always been my lifeline. Fortunately, I brought my sewing machine. I never went anywhere without my sewing machine. It is certainly true that if I had been offered diamonds or a sewing machine, I would have opted for my sewing machine. It would have been more sensible to take the diamond and buy a ticket out, but nobody offered me a diamond, and I had a sewing machine. Sewing got me through some bad times.

I took out a subscription to *Vogue Pattern Book*, and it eventually arrived. Then I wrote to my mother, trying to describe the material I wanted, and she went to Liberty's and tried to buy suitable cotton. Fortunately, my mother had pretty good taste, so there wasn't much that was totally useless; and boredom and desperation can induce amazing feats of artistic endeavour. I usually ended up with a new dress or something. Of course, she had to send the sewing cotton, too, and the zips and buttons, and it took weeks for things to arrive.

Servants came largely from the subcontinent and would come to Abu Dhabi only if they were too incompetent to get a job anywhere else because there was nothing for them to do in their free time. Occasionally, one from Dubai could be tempted because he needed the money, but these people didn't last long. In Dubai there was a proper cinema, a bazaar, and coffee shops where they could meet up with their friends, so none of them could resist the temptations for more than a month or so before returning there. The cost of living was extremely high for them, too, much higher than Dubai, so even though they were better paid, they were not happy.

There was one only one other place to shop for food, and that was Mr Bhojraj. This entrepreneurial Indian had the only grocery shop in 'town'. The first time I visited I discovered that his shelves contained anything you could want—within reason—for a cocktail party, but nothing for normal eating. Before I arrived, the two English families living there had access to supplies from the oil companies, who flew in everything they needed several times a week. I was especially jealous of the bread. I laboured long and hard to learn to make bread, and of course there were no bread mixes, so I started with yeast and flour. When I finally did get it to raise my husband opened a door and slammed it so it all collapsed. I never ever managed to make good bread.

The bachelors just ate whatever their servants would dish up. This usually meant putting a tin of peas and tinned pie in the oven on a low heat before they walked to the souk, where they gossiped for as long as possible before walking back. They were, of course, walking through thick sand in temperatures of over one hundred degrees for maybe half a mile, so it didn't do to complain too much. In the evening the men got together and ate cocktail sausages and nuts washed down by any available alcohol.

So Mr Bhojraj and I came to an agreement. He was keen to increase his inventory but he didn't know what to get. The bank in its wisdom had agreed that every three months I could fly to Bahrain and fill packing cases with things like Milton for baby bottles, Cow & Gate baby milk, any kind of food that would survive a couple of weeks on a dhow in high temperatures, and anything we needed for the house. Lots of things that were not available in Dubai were available in Bahrain because of the size of the communities, but my agreement with Mr Bhojraj was that any empty tin or container could be taken to him, and he would try to find it in Dubai and stock it. It worked well for both of us. His business improved, and our diet became a bit more varied.

CHAPTER 13

WATER CONTINUED TO be a problem, and I still have a sensitive ear for a running tap. All drinking water had to be boiled and then poured into a filter which had three candles made of kind of porous stone. I never bothered to find out what kind of stone it was but after a week the candles had to be removed and they had certainly gathered a lot of strange matter. This was scrubbed off and the filter washed out. The water from the filter was poured into glass bottles and stored in the fridge. At this stage I am not sure how much good this all did. The boiling certainly helped to kill off a few bugs but the bottles of water were certainly not sterile and were simply refilled when empty. It was of course not possible to buy commercially bottled water.

As the population grew, the man with the donkey couldn't cope, so some bright entrepreneur in Dubai started to put huge tanks on the back of his truck, filled them with water, and drove it across the desert to Abu Dhabi. Not an easy drive, and the price reflected the problems, but he became much in demand, and the business took off. The water was pumped into a tank on the roof of the house, where it got very hot. So the immersion heater inside the house, never turned on, became a source of cold water to temper the boiling water that came from the roof tank. Heaven help a visitor who left a tap running. It could mean no water for washing or showers for a couple of days until another tanker driver could be induced to drive from Dubai; and this was when tanker drivers got hijacked by desperate people.

There was a small distillation plant, but this was inadequate; and with the influx of people a bigger plant was needed. Abu Dhabi was starting to get lots of oil money, and Sheikh Shahkbut was being persuaded to put money into the infrastructure of the State. A subqua road was being built along the shoreline, and a proper jetty built rather than the rather shaky structure that ran off the beach. This meant it was possible to go for a short walk, something impossible in soft sand. However, it never got good enough to push a pram, although I did try it on one occasion.

Colonel Sir John Edmond Hugh Boustead, KBE, CMG, DSO, MC & Bar became the Political Agent in 1961. He had had an amazing career. Born in 1895, he was getting on a bit by the time he got to us. He deserted from the navy in the First World War to join the army so he could fight in the Crimea and eventually was granted a Queen's Pardon. He had been commander of the Sudan Camel Corps, and there was a rumour he formed the Hadrami Bedouin Legion. He captained the British team in the 1920 summer Olympics in the modern pentathlon, and was a seasoned explorer. He also brought with him his own standards of behaviour, somewhat Victorian, which were beginning to go out of fashion. He was the Queen's representative, so when he stood up everyone stood up, and no one sat until he sat. There was only one place for him at a dinner party, on the right of the hostess and woe betide anyone who got it wrong. And of course no one left a party before he did. He suited Abu Dhabi perfectly with its mixed bag of inhabitants, although I think he caused the Foreign Office a few problems.

He liked to entertain, and would often invite more people to dinner than he had room for. This meant that just before dinner someone would have to whisper in the ear of the least important guests that there was a problem, and they had to make a discreet exit. They were frequently happy to do so, since the Colonel's dining room was not air-conditioned, and most of the year it was hot, with only a damp breeze blowing through it. Dress was always fairly formal, and his cook left a lot to be desired.

He lived above the offices, as we had, but he was a little careless with his confidential papers. On breezy days everyone would be sent scurrying around the compound to fetch the most secret, for-his-eyes-only documents he had been studying on the balcony when the a breeze blew up.

Accommodation continued to be a problem. If you had a spare room, it was likely to be in great demand. So a hotel was hurriedly built, and this brought in more people. Suddenly this tiny place with hardly any locals and few expatriates was awash with politicians, architects, and writers.

There was still not much to do but socialise in the evenings, and this usually meant drinking. Gin was cheaper than Windolene, better at cleaning windows, and easier to find, but not the best thing for the bachelor community that was growing. The community as a whole was aged between 23 and 35, and whereas married couples usually had children and accommodation not too bad by local standards, the bachelors lived in tiny flats and had nothing to do but quarrel — or perhaps try to seduce one of the wives, which was a popular game. The place was full of eligible and attractive young men. Nick Hartley, Duncan Slater, Alan Fosler, and Hugh Carol were all active on the party scene, and with an increasing number of pretty, young, bored wives, there was a lot of temptation.

In time some of the married couples brought in nannies to help look after the children. Heather, Carolyn, and Helen all descended on the community. These were young English girls who were suffering broken hearts, looking for husbands or just wanted to see a bit of the world. I'm sure they didn't expect to find Abu Dhabi as primitive as it was, but since they were so much in demand by the bachelors, they seemed to have a pretty good time.

In the end we brought in a servant from India. I wrote to friends there and asked if they could look around and find someone for me; I was pretty desperate. There was nothing unusual in this. Pay in the Gulf was much higher than in India, and many servants were keen to come. They sent nearly all their salary home because they were housed and fed by their employers, and the really clever ones managed to buy property in their villages with their salaries. The idea was that your friends in India would interview them, and they would try them out as a cook, then send the information to us. They came up with a name, and we completed all the formalities, which were long and expensive in the true manner of Indian bureaucrats—in fact all bureaucrats. After several weeks Martin arrived, and seemed like a pleasant man; and he was, but it turned out he had never cooked in his life. He had been working as a car salesman in Bombay.

It had been an expensive business bringing him in. But he was keen and I was desperate, so with the help of Mrs Beeton I taught him to cook. The good thing was that he could read and was intelligent. The other good thing was that he learned to cook the way I cooked, and had not picked up any bad habits from previous employers. I never asked my friends how they managed to send me a car salesman when I asked for a cook.

Chapter 14

One evening we were having a dinner party at which Bob Arnold was a guest. He was a very sociable man, but even he was getting tired of the endless stream of young men on his doorstep every evening. 'We should find somewhere for them to go. We should start a club.' A great idea but hard to follow up. However, the idea didn't die, and after many more 'meetings' Bob came up with an idea to get the community interested. After a lot of hard work on the part of Bob and his wife and us, a mysterious pirate party was organised in the desert to prove that it was possible. Everyone dressed up with what was on hand. Pirate costumes, we decided, could be conjured out of almost anything. It was all going well until a shamal blew up and wrecked the barbeque. Sand was everywhere. Fortunately one of the guests had enough clout to ensure that the hotel took us in despite the protests of the Greek manager. And the party continued indoors.

It brought the community together and got the attention of the oil companies who were moving lots of people into the area. It forced attention on the lack of facilities, and it generated enough enthusiasm to get Abu Dhabi Petroleum Company (ADPC) on board, who gave us the lease of a derelict old house way out of town so it would not annoy the locals. Colonel Boustead, the Political Agent, saw how important it was that there be some sort of centre for people to get together, so he got Sheikh Shakhbut to give it his blessing — or at least he did not oppose it. It was to be called 'The Club', a name which could offend no one.

ADPC gave us the house known as 'Henderson's Folly', named after the oil engineer who had built and lived in it from time to time. It had no electricity, no water, and only a sand track up to it, but the bachelors like Cliff Leslie got tanker drivers to deliver water, and one of the oil companies donated an old generator and got people to fix it up. It was in everyone's interest to find a place where people could go.

In time we built a tennis court and a paved area where the first Abu Dhabi Poppy Ball was held. We danced on sandy concrete paving stones, and dress code was 'formal': Gulf rig (black dress trousers with a short sleeved white shirt and a cummerbund) for the men and long dresses for the women. Everyone contributed food of some kind, the evening was a success, and Treasurer Alan Ashmole was able to send the British Legion a bit more money for its coffers.

CHAPTER 15

AFTER A YEAR or so the bank decided it was going to build a proper bank building to replace the hole in the wall it had been using, a proper building with proper security, built on the site of our current house; so once again we had to move out. But as usual there was nowhere for us to go. The bank was not good at thinking these things through. Hamish Neelan, who worked for African Eastern, and his wife Di lived near what was to be the site of our new house, and they offered us a spare room—noble of them, since they were newly married, and we had a child and a dog.

Fortunately it doesn't take long to tear down a prefab, patch it together, and put it up again. So within a couple of weeks we were reinstalled further out of town in what looked like a badly wrapped parcel; but it was home.

One of the downsides was that we had just installed a telephone in our old house, but the line did not then stretch to the new house. The bank also was going to build a permanent house in the compound. It spent a fortune on high walls around it and a concrete drive linking it to the subqua road so that it was possible to get in and out without being stuck in the sand. It meant that the compound was full of workmen all the time, and there were all sorts of tools just lying around in the sand—not ideal with a small, adventurous boy around. Ine day he found a rough ladder and was halfway to the roof before someone spotted him.

The bank then decided they would build a bigger prefabricated house for us next door to the old one. Neville thought this was a bad idea. Everyone else lived in proper concrete houses, and he thought another prefabricated house would reflect badly on the bank, suggesting it gave the impression the bank was not sure it was staying in Abu Dhabi. No one was building prefabricated house for staff anymore. Following lots of exchanges of letters, management got cross, and we were told to proceed on leave almost immediately, and then return to Bahrain, where Neville would be number three in the bank. They knew how to make their point. Management knew best.

CHAPTER 16

LEAVE IN THE UK was good, but living with parents with a child for more than a short while can be a bit trying for all concerned. My mother was very helpful, but her life was not our life, and six months in the North during a very cold winter convinced me we needed a house of our own — farther south.

We were in the UK for six months in 1963. We were there during the Cuban Missile Crisis; the jailing of Nelson Mandela, whose resistance organisation was then known as the Spear of the Nation, and who was regarded as a terrorist; and the Profumo Affair had just begun its rumblings. I began to feel that living in Abu Dhabi without instant news had been rather a blessing.

We came back from a leave where Jeremy had had his first experience of snow and his first experience of fresh food, which he was not at all sure he liked. It was the start of all kinds of eating problems.

So I arrived in Bahrain again, this time to stay. Jeremy was almost three.

Bahrain is an island nation in what was the Persian Gulf when we lived there, and is now the Arabian Gulf. The only way to get there was by air or sea, and the causeway which now joins it to Saudi Arabia had not been constructed. But it was an old civilisation, and because of its position as a trading nation, from pearls in 600 BC to oil exploration in 1957, it had a sophisticated population. The British had been much in evidence, and with oil came roads and schools. We went from sand tracks and pushing Land Rovers to an MG sports car on dual carriageways. There were hairdressers; mini department stores with toys, clothes, and cosmetics; as well as a souk selling all kinds of jewellery, clothing and food. Bahrain had a large multinational population when we were there, but it still had a British Resident who worked closely with the Ruler, Sheikh Essa, to protect British interests.

This time there was a house. We moved into Nabeel Gardens, a little enclave of a dozen houses and a swimming pool. Jeremy needed companionship, so I found a nursery school run by a fierce American woman, and off he went. She gave me a run-down on his character—with which I totally disagreed, of course—but maybe she was right. I spent the whole morning sitting by the phone in tears and waiting for it to ring so I could go and bring Jeremy home, but the morning passed, and I picked him up looking not too unhappy.

We brought Martin the cook up from Abu Dhabi, and that made life easier. He was happy to be kept on, and had become a good cook, did the washing and ironing, and only complained when he did not have enough to do. In Bahrain there was an active Catholic community, but as in Abu Dhabi, once the church was built, Martin had to contribute ten per cent of his salary to the church, and he found this very hard.

Neville was the accountant in Bahrain—number three on the totem pole. It had quite a number of British staff since in Bahrain the Eastern Bank was the number one bank. It banked the ruler Sheikh Essa, and so the locals trusted it.

Bahrain had a large British community. There was a naval base with several ships and some sort of army base where apparently the wives rented themselves out to local rich Arabs and came into the bank with wads of cash to be remitted to the UK. This did create some sort of a problem when I walked along the street, because taxi drivers would suggest all kinds of ways I could make extra money.

Apart from this Bahrain was an easy place to live. There was a proper school, shops, paved roads, electricity, and water on tap. Bahrain also had more of a winter than Abu Dhabi, so for a couple of months it was cooler and we could switch off the air conditioning. We lived in a bungalow that had a garden where I grew tomatoes and other vegetables. My zinnias were the envy of my neighbour. I had an MG sports car in British racing green, not a very sensible car when the sun beat down on your head, but I was still youngish, and the car was fun. Eventually Jeremy moved on to St. Christopher's school, and after school we would drive out to the ruler's beach, which Sheikh Essa allowed the European community to use. The beach had tables and chairs, and English afternoon tea appeared on large trays on the days when Essa came.

Sheikh Essa also gave wonderfully glamorous dinner parties at his palace, where everyone dressed up but did not actually eat much. They started at 6:30 in the evening and were over by 8:00 p.m., so they didn't get in the way of any other activities that might be planned.

I learned to play bridge taught by some kind and patient friends, and I remembered them every time we moved to a new country and had to make friends. Although bridge is not always a friendly game, knowing how to play did mean I would often be invited to make up a four. Bridge players are always looking for a fourth player, so I played a lot of systems in a lot of countries, which makes me a rather difficult partner in the UK, where everyone plays Acol and thinks it the only reliable system.

Some of the best bridge players I met were Arabs. If they didn't invent it, they certainly took it up with enthusiasm. In the beginning I found it unnerving when they would put down their cards after two rounds and say they had made their contract. I learned not to argue, since they would sigh and explain it all to me very slowly and they were always right.

In 1965 we decided it was time for Jeremy to have a sister. Bahrain had good hospitals and many doctors, so it would not be a problem. It meant I had to give up my beloved sports car when I could no longer get behind the wheel and move on to a mini traveller. That's when I realised middle age was approaching.

All went well until I was six months pregnant and the Bank suddenly decided that they could not find anyone else who could face living in Abu Dhabi. It appeared that one officer had 'got religion' and had begun trying to convert people to Christianity. The Bank was worried about repercussions, so we were posted back. Obviously more important than the fact that I was six months pregnant, and there were still no health facilities in Abu Dhabi. 'We don't employ the wives.' Was the cry as of old.

It was a particularly stressful time because Martin the cook had discovered the delights of beer. I assume it was beer. Liquor licences were given out according to the level of one's salary. Low-paid workers were allowed only enough units to buy beer, whereas chairmen of companies who had to entertain had a very generous allowance. Anyway, Martin began to get very drunk, and just when I needed him most to help with the packing and moving, he had to be sent back to India.

Medical care had not improved in Abu Dhabi, although there was now a doctor there, Dr Desmond McCauley. His reputation was well known throughout the Gulf as a man who, if he told you that you were going to die, was never wrong. He meant well, although his medical knowledge, gained in Ireland many decades earlier, was hardly up-to-date. On the other hand, during our first tour in Abu Dhabi, Jeremy had been very ill with some stomach complaint, and although everyone tried to help, including the doctors on Das Island via the radio, he just got worse. Fortunately someone contacted Desmond, who was out in the desert doing his rounds. He appeared on my doorstep, took one look, prodded a bit, and such was his experience of the local bugs that he knew exactly what to prescribe. Within a week Jeremy was back to normal.

Even so, going back to Abu Dhabi to give birth did not seem like a good idea. My first child had to be induced, and it seemed highly possible that the second would be equally reluctant to enter the world. I also had the example of a friend who had lost a baby in Makulah—which did have a hospital—because they waited too long.

CHAPTER 17

So it was back to my long-suffering mother again in June 1966, hanging around, and trying to amuse a very energetic small boy in a tiny flat. I managed to get him into school, which helped, but then he fell off his tricycle. I have to confess I was not sure there was a problem, but when he winced on raising his arm, I drove him to hospital and sure enough he had fractured his collar bone. When he came back from having it strapped up, the nurses were all laughing. 'Apparently you cannot go home unless the baby is a girl,' one of them said. I had no idea what the baby was going to be, in 1966 that was common. I had never heard of scans, even if they had been invented by then. I just wanted the baby to arrive.

Because I had not given my mother much warning of my arrival it was difficult for her to find me a place in a maternity ward but she managed it but was told I would only be able to stay thirtysix hours. My children were always reluctant to enter the world, so again the baby had to be induced and time was running out. I went in by taxi on the third of August at 9:30 a.m. Hospitals always assumed I was a single mother since I never managed to produce a worried husband or any other kind. Fortunately, I had produced a daughter. The nurse asked me her name. My mind went blank, and out came, 'Amanda Jane'. Half an hour later, when the drugs had worn off, I said, 'Oh it was supposed to be Alyson Joy, but forget it. Amanda is a much nicer name.' This, however, did cause some confusion when Neville put an announcement in the *Times* saying it was Alyson Joy, and I put one in the *Telegraph* saying it was Amanda Jane. I felt I should have the last word.

Thirty-six hours, our GP told me, was as long as they would keep me, and so the next morning my mother brought Jeremy to the hospital to pick me up. I could not believe what I saw. Jeremy's face was swollen and he had a plug up one nostril. Apparently when I left the flat his nose started to bleed and wouldn't stop; she finally had to take him to a doctor to have the nostril cauterised. I felt really bad because I know what a horrible business that is. We both suffered from really bad nosebleeds from time to time, and no one knows why.

Anyway, Jeremy was delighted to have a sister, and we took Amanda back to the flat, making it even more congested than before. That night, having just settled both Jeremy and Amanda, the phone rang. The operator told me I had a telegram—remember this was 1966, when such things still existed. She said the telegram read 'Everything alright, don't worry'. I was too tired to be cross but was irritated. Why should I worry? I had enough on my plate, and as far as I knew Neville was having a lovely time at a party celebrating the birth of his daughter. He might have a hangover, but that was hardly life threatening.

It turned out that Neville, in his usual confident fashion had organised a party to celebrate the birth of his new child. He had no idea whether it would be a boy or a girl. Abu Dhabi was very small, so if anyone was having a party, everyone came, including visitors, and on that occasion there were a lot of people visiting the Political Agency. Apparently they kept rushing off into corners and having serious discussions. The next morning they got hold of Sheikh Shakhbut and told him he had to abdicate. He had large amounts of money, but was not spending it fast enough on schools and public services. His brother had promised to spend the wealth on roads and schools and on bringing Abu Dhabi into the twentieth century. Sheikh Shakhbut had always maintained that unless he kept careful control, the money would go to outsiders who organised the new contracts and not the people of Abu Dhabi. Sheikh Shakhbut may have just been an untravelled desert sheikh, but he knew all about corruption and could spot it a mile off, as he proved time and time again. The coup meant that all communication to the outside world was cut off—except, of course, the BBC reported it on their early morning news. It was certainly the most dramatic and exciting day that Abu Dhabi had ever had until then.

With a thirty-six-hour-old baby and a small boy of five, I really did not have a lot of time to worry about anything else. Very little sleep meant very little time to worry. We stayed on in the UK for six weeks, and it could have been longer, since I woke up one morning thinking the end had come. I had developed renal colic. It was extremely painful, and I insisted that my mother call our family doctor. He was sympathetic and fed me morphine, which at least killed the pain. I told him I didn't have time to get ill since I was due to drive to London in a week and catch a plane to Abu Dhabi. He shook his head in disbelief at this madness. He had ever left England only to go fishing in Scotland, and as he constantly told my mother, could not understand my life. Fortunately the pain subsided, and I suppose the stone passed. It proved a useful experience later on when Neville developed the same condition and Dr Desmond Hawley asked me what I thought it was. I had no trouble diagnosing his symptoms, and Desmond agreed and shipped Neville up to Bahrain for a week.

CHAPTER 18

I LOADED THE children, my mother, and piles of luggage into a mini traveller and drove south to Heathrow Airport to catch my plane, first to Bahrain, where Neville was due to meet us, before catching another plane the next day to Abu Dhabi. On disembarking, eager to show off the new daughter as ordered, I was met by Peter Burfoot. A General Manager had arrived in Abu Dhabi from London, the same one who had told me that unless I accompanied Neville to Abu Dhabi with my first baby, the Bank would not pay my airfare. They were not paying it this time either. But this meant Neville had to stay in Abu Dhabi, so Peter had been drafted in to look after me until the next day's plane. Not too many bachelors could have coped as well as Peter, who was generosity itself with the chaos I caused in his beautifully appointed flat.

The next day we got on the plane to Abu Dhabi, and now there was a more organised airport although nothing like today's of course. Neville met us off the plane and we drove home to meet up with Mr. Goldsmith the General Manager. Mr Goldsmith looking rather sheepish suggested that he was probably rather unpopular with me. In some circumstances not responding to a stupid remark is the best answer.

This time we moved into a larger prefabricated house that had been erected while we were in Bahrain. Lots had changed while we had been away; the population had multiplied several times over. Several British families had moved in during.1966. The expatriate population was still mainly British and Indian. Every nationality was represented, but the engineers for the new roads and the new airport and all the new houses and offices were by and large British.

Everything had changed. The days when I was welcomed into the majlis were gone. No more sitting surrounded by tribesmen with guns, drinking *gahwa*, as Arabic coffee was known.

It was one huge building site. This time at least we had a house, and we inherited the cook and the sweeper from our predecessors, which made life easier.

There was a visiting Church of England minister, so we had Amanda christened. There was no Protestant church, so the christening took place in our house. I discovered that it was possible to fly in flowers from Doha for the ceremony. This may not seem much, but there were still no flowers in Abu Dhabi because there was still a shortage of water. It was not a question of donkeys anymore. There was a huge distillation plant, but it still was not something one took for granted and water was still being delivered by tanker and boiled and filtered.

Abu Dhabi still had one thing to throw at us. In 1967 during the winter a shamal blew up. This was the wind that blew from the north that brought temperatures down and often great sandstorms from across the Gulf. The tide came in, and pushed by the wind, inch by inch it crept up the beach. I had never seen the sea so high. It began to ooze across the dirt road and became less interesting and more anxiety-making, and worse when it swept into the compound and dislodged the six-foot wall surrounding it and forcing it to fall over. Then it crossed the wide stretch of sand in the compound and attacked the new concrete driveway that immediately buckled, leaving wide cracks. It took seconds for it to start seeping into the house, where Jeremy was happily enjoying the eight inches of water in his bedroom and watching the rugs float.

We had been told by the Political Agency that if we ever needed assistance, we should tie a white sheet to our front door—a statement that always baffled me. Since our house was now sitting in the middle of the sea, it seemed unreasonable to tie a sheet and hope for a boat, so when Alistair Macaskill appeared, having parked his Land Rover on a high sand dune behind the house, and suggested it was time to leave, we evacuated via the back way and climbed over the generator house roof like lost castaways: Jeremy, Amanda, Neville, and of course me with a few things packed. At the time the ADMA general manager was Chris Willy, and he and his wife kindly offered us a bed until we could sort ourselves out.

By then there was a hotel, although the manager was not keen on families. Bachelors were easier. Anyway, we were able to stay there for a week while the sea went down and our house dried out. But the locals who were living in *barustis* had a bad time because the weather stayed cold and overcast for several days. The whole of our part of the town stayed flooded, and the local inhabitants had no means of drying clothes or anything else.

On June 6 Jeremy had his sixth birthday party on the beach in front of the house. It was the day after the Israeli-Arab Six-Day War started, but we never let little things like that get in the way. There was a lot of tension because there were a multitude of Palestinians living in Dubai, and many of them were very angry and were marching around, trying to find a way to get to Palestine quickly to join in the fight. Of course, by the time the would-be warriors did the paperwork the war was over, in just six days, so we could all settle down again. But we did keep a bag packed.

For the next year we watched Abu Dhabi grow like a mushroom. Hundreds of new people moved in, most of them employed by the oil industry in one way or another. but with Sheikh Shakhbut gone, the purse strings were opened, and huge projects were entered into. Contractors were everywhere. A huge new port was created for all the stuff that had to be shipped in by sea because that was really the only practical way to bring in heavy equipment and food. Spinney's opened a cold store where it was possible to buy a variety of frozen food, including ice cream for the first time. The Club was booming, as was the hotel, but it was hard for anyone to find a place to stay.

A whole estate of houses was created by Iraq Petroleum Company IPC behind a high brick wall. As usual, they had their own little community, and mostly the people who lived there stayed behind it. But a few entered the mainstream social life and joined in the parties. The tight little community began to break up, and most of the people who had been there in the early sixties were due for a posting. Everything was changing at such a rate it was confusing. It was no longer possible to invite everyone when you had a party. In the beginning, contractors, policemen, plumbers, and bankers could all mix up, particularly at Christmas. But as the numbers grew, the community divided, and everyone moved into the circle in which they were most comfortable. I don't think it was deliberate; it was just natural. The Bank decided we could have a small boat and a tennis court for recreation, but the boat was still on a ship from England, and the tennis court was half finished when we left.

Flies were a terrible problem as the town grew. They would cover anything that didn't move in a few minutes. They were particularly attracted to children's mouths and noses. The cooler the weather, the more flies there were; and whereas winter was very pleasant, the only way Amanda, still a few months old, could be protected from them was to have a fly-netted cage built. There she could lie and kick and doze in peace while the flies covered the outside looking for a gap in the screens.

Amanda hated sand, which was rather unfortunate, since we were surrounded by it. The only place to go was the beach, where she would sit firmly on a rug, complaining if even a few grains of sand came near her. For this reason she showed no inclination to walk, but indoors she would crawl everywhere.

A small school opened, so Jeremy could get some kind of education and at least a chance to play with the other children who were starting to arrive.

Neville went down with renal colic, and was shipped up to Bahrain to have his stone examined. I was about to pop Jeremy into the bath one night when I got a shock from the water. Fortunately, I had tried the temperature with my hand. I rang a friend who came around and confirmed that somehow electricity had seeped into the bath, which resulted in another urgent call to a friend who knew about plumbing and electricity. I could almost guarantee that the minute Neville left for any reason, the Gods thought it was time to have a good laugh at my expense; but I was getting used to it. On another occasion, when Neville was in Bahrain with suspected bilharzias, one of the men working on the tennis court attempted to kidnap Jeremy, but that's another story.

We left Abu Dhabi in late 1967. Our tennis court in the compound was half-finished, and on the horizon we could see the ship that contained the small motorboat we had been promised. Amanda was just over a year old and refusing to walk in case she touched the sand. Abu Dhabi was one large building site, but now there was a hospital, we had telephone, and a huge distillation plant made the problem of water less urgent.

The Club that we had initiated was going well, and the oil companies gave it their support to improve the facilities. We left to go on leave and then to Bombay, but the Bank changed it's mind and we went on to wars, revolutions, arson attacks and civil disturbances, all in the name of Banking.

So we went to our goodbye parties and said farewell to our friends. It was all a bit sad, since I felt we had been a small part of the growth of the town. It had gone from being a village to a town in the blink of an eye. Today it's a huge city—all in fifty years. Our Land Rover drove along what was still a dirt road, and on every side were cranes and labourers from the subcontinent. Friends came to see us off, and we left for the UK on another small plane. The airport was still just a windsock in the desert, but now there was passport control and a customs officer.

I sometimes felt Abu Dhabi had 'stolen my wits away', but on other occasions I was definitely 'crazed with the spell of far Arabia' — something the poet and writer Walter de la Mare obviously understood.

I hope anyone who reads this book will find it interesting and informative. I read a lot of biographies but of course they are mostly about men who have changed history. Few women change the big picture and details of domestic life in the past are overlooked. This book is about domestic life in the Gulf in the early 1960s before oil revenues started rolling in.

We have been back to Abu Dhabi a couple of times, in recent years but it is a different country now, and impossible to track the places we once worked and played but it must certainly be an easier place to live.